I'm thinking of you on your special day. . .
and I'm wishing you the best of everything the future holds.

_____
To

_____
From

_____
On This Date

A
Birthday
Celebration

I'm So Glad God Made You!

Ellyn Sanna

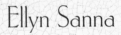

A DayMaker Greeting Book

Enjoy Your Special Day!

Most of us can remember

    a time when a birthday—

especially if it was one's own—

brightened the world as if

    a second sun had risen.

ROBERT LYND

I'm **remembering** you on your **birthday**——

and wishing you a **sun-filled** day.

It is **lovely** when I forget all birthdays,

including my own,

to find that somebody **remembers** me.

ELLEN GLASGOW

Life is so full of meaning and purpose,

so full of beauty,

beneath its covering that you will find

that earth but cloaks your heaven.

FRA GIOVANNI

May you
celebrate the
many blessings
God has given you.

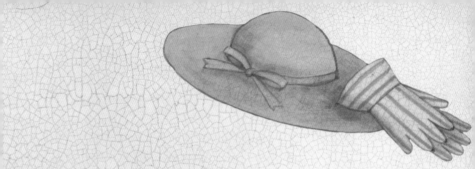

Let us acknowledge all good,

all delight that the world holds, and be content.

GEORGE MACDONALD

One of the secrets of a happy life
is continuous small treats.

IRIS MURDOCH

On your birthday—

and all year round—

I pray that your life will be

chock-full of special moments.

Take time to enjoy life.

Don't be so busy

you forget to notice

a sunset or

a child's smile.

And be good to yourself.

There is something in every season, in every day,

to celebrate with thanksgiving.

GLORIA GAITHER

May you celebrate all
the possibilities of your day!

Every day we live is
a priceless gift of God,
loaded with possibilities
to learn something new,
to gain fresh insights.

DALE EVANS ROGERS

Celebrate Yourself!

You are a unique creation of God.

In all the world,

there's no one else like you. . . .

Praise God for all the gifts

He gave the world

when He created you.

Our God gives you everything you need,
makes you everything you're to be.

2 THESSALONIANS 1:2 THE MESSAGE

What lies behind us and

what lies before us

are tiny matters compared to

what lies within us.

RALPH WALDO EMERSON

One of the greatest steps

in discovering who we are

is discovering who God is. . . .

Who we are in Christ is everything.

SHEILA WALSH

Since you are like no other being

ever created since the beginning of time,

you are incomparable.

BRENDA UELAND

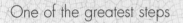

You are God's created beauty and
the focus of His affection and delight.

JANET L. WEAVER

Our selves may be imperfect, incapable,
and weak, but our souls. . .
are the image of the living God.

MARY HOLLINGSWORTH

Grace means God

accepts me just as I am.

He does not require

or insist that I measure up to

someone else's standard of performance.

He loves me completely,

thoroughly, and perfectly.

There's nothing I can do

to add or detract from that love.

MARY GRAHAM

You are **precious** to God,

and today He celebrates your **life**.

Why not join the celebration?

Rest in the **assurance** that God is

doing great things in your life.

Know that you are loved and

treasured by the **Creator** of the universe.

I'm so glad God made you!

Take Pleasure in Your Age!

God has new things

to show you at every age;

He has delights and insights,

wonders and fulfillment planned

for each year of your life.

So take pleasure in the age

you are right now.

It's the perfect age for you to be.

Indeed, now that I come to think of it,

I never really feel grown-up at all.

Perhaps this is because childhood,

catching our imagination when it is fresh and tender,

never lets go of us.

J. B. PRIESTLEY

Childhood is the world

of miracle and wonder:

as if creation rose, bathed in light,

out of darkness,

utterly new and fresh and astonishing.

The end of childhood is

when things cease to astonish us.

When the world seems familiar,

when one has got used to existence,

one has become an adult.

EUGÉNE IONESCO

Time always seems long to the child. . .

when he surrenders his whole soul to

each moment of a happy day.

DAG HAMMARSKJOLD

Oh, the wild joys of living!
the leaping from rock to rock. . .

ROBERT BROWNING

The story of living goes on perpetually.

The days and the years inevitably turn the pages

and open new chapters.

LILIAN WHITING

Our LORD speaks simply: . . .

"Trust Me to pour My love through thee,

as minute succeeds minute."

AMY CARMICHAEL

Don't rob yourself

of the joy of this season

by wishing you were

in a future or past one.

CHERYL BIEHL

Consider the lilies how they grow.

LUKE 12:27 KJV

Keep the sky clear.
Open wide every avenue of your being
to receive the blessed influences
your Divine Husbandman may
bring to bear upon you.
Bask in the sunshine of His love.
Drink of the waters of His goodness.
Keep your face upturned to Him
as the flowers do to the sun.
Look, and your soul
shall live and grow.

HANNAH WHITALL SMITH

Treasure the Years
That Have Passed!

Your birthday is a good day to look back at the years that

have passed and reflect on all that God has done in your life.

Notice the patterns He created over the years.

Celebrate the memories of love that fill your life.

Rejoice in the years' achievements.

May your memories

be birthday gifts of joy.

When we recall the past,

we usually find that it is the simplest things—

not the great occasions—

that in retrospect give off

the greatest glow of happiness.

BOB HOPE

Memories are perhaps the best gifts of all.

GLORIA GAITHER

We do not remember days,

we remember moments.

Make moments worth remembering.

CASARE PAVASE

It is well to drop the old
that one may seize the new.

LILIAN WHITING

Treasure your memories today—

but don't linger in the past,

mourning for the "good old days."

God's presence was with you

each moment of those days,

and I know He filled your life with blessings—

but He is also with you today.

And He has a storehouse

of blessing He still waits

to give you in the future.

Christ Jesus has bags of mercy

that have never even been opened.

That is why the Bible says

He has goodness laid up. . . .

Who knows what will happen if

He opens just one more of these bags.

JOHN BUNYAN

Wishing You a Future
Piled High with Gifts!

"For I know the plans I have for you," declares the LORD,

"plans to prosper you and not to harm you,

plans to give you hope and a future."

JEREMIAH 29:11 NIV

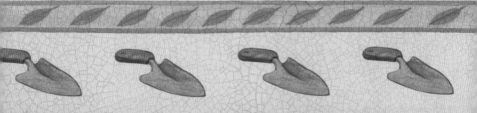

Face the future
with joy and anticipation.
God has great plans for you!

I don't know what the future holds,

but I know who holds the future.

E. STANLEY JONES

Always begin anew with the day,

just as nature does;

it is one of the sensible things

that nature does.

GEORGE E. WOODBERRY

Fill up the crevices of time
    with the things that matter most.

AMY CARMICHAEL

If we celebrate the years behind us

they become stepping-stones

of strength and joy

for the years ahead.

ANONYMOUS

I love to think that God appoints

My portion day by day;

Events of life are in His hand,

And I would only say,

Appoint them in Thine own good time,

And in Thine own best way.

A. L. WARING

The LORD will guide you always;

he will **satisfy** your needs. . . .

You will be like a well-watered **garden**,

like a **spring** whose waters never fail.

ISAIAH 58:11 NIV

God will never, never, never let us down

if we have faith and put our trust in Him.

He will always look after us.

MOTHER TERESA

Trust in the LORD with all your heart and

lean not on your own understanding;

in all your ways acknowledge him,

and he will make your paths straight.

PROVERBS 3:5–6 NIV

There are better things ahead
than any we leave behind.

C. S. LEWIS

Surely goodness and love

will follow me

all the days of my life,

and I will dwell in the house

of the LORD forever.

PSALM 23:6 NIV

No eye has seen,

nor ear heard,

nor the human heart conceived,

what God has prepared

for those who love him.

1 CORINTHIANS 2:9 NRSV

Think of your birthday as a **promise** from God. Imagine Him speaking the words of Psalm 139 (paraphrased) directly to your heart:

"Look, My child, see what I have created?
Before you were ever born, I knew you.
I knit you together in your mother's womb,
making you complex and perfect;
My workmanship was marvelous! Before your birth,
I recorded every day of your life in My book;
I laid out the moments and filled them full of blessings.
Those past moments were My gift to you—but I have more gifts
I long to give you. For I both precede and follow you;
I place My hand of blessing on your head as
I lead you along the path of everlasting life.
My thoughts of you are precious to Me.
You will never be separated from My spirit."

I wish you sunshine on
your path and storms
to season your journey.
I wish you peace—
in the world in which you live
and in the smallest corner
of the heart where truth is kept.
I wish you faith—
to help define your living and your life.
More I cannot wish you—
except perhaps love—
to make all the rest worthwhile.

ROBERT A. WARD

It is God to whom and with whom we travel,

and while He is the End of our journey,

He is also at every stopping place.

ELISABETH ELLIOT

Time is a precious gift of God;
so precious that it's only given to us
moment by moment.

AMELIA BARR

Time with your heavenly Father

is never wasted.

EMILIE BARNES

The LORD is faithful to all his promises
and loving toward all he has made.

PSALM 145:13 NIV

Trust in the LORD with all your heart;

do not depend on your own understanding.

Seek his will in all you do,

and he will direct your paths.

PROVERBS 3:5–6 NLT

Take delight in the LORD,
	and he will give you
	your heart's desires.

PSALM 37:4 NLT

He is first, and He is last!

And we are gathered up in between,

as in great arms of eternal lovingkindness.

AMY CARMICHAEL

"I am Alpha and Omega,
the first and the last."

REVELATION 1:11 KJV

The LORD will go

before you,

the God of Israel

will be your rear guard.

ISAIAH 52:12 NIV

We see hardly one inch

of the narrow lane of time.

To our God,

eternity lies open as a meadow.

AMY CARMICHAEL

I will answer them before they even call to me.

While they are still talking to me about their needs,

I will go ahead and answer their prayers!

ISAIAH 65:24 NLT

Occasionally I must remind myself

that all gifts are given to me,

God's beloved child,

with incomparable love and joy. . . .

Everything good and loving in life

has its source in God,

including all gifts.

MARILYN MEBERG

As you enjoy your gifts today,

remember—

the greatest gift of all is the gift of love!

Lord, may no gift of Yours ever

take Your place in my heart.

Help me to hold them lightly

in an open palm.

ELISABETH ELLIOT

I wish you all the joy that you can wish.

WILLIAM SHAKESPEARE

Please know my **heart** is filled

with **thoughts** of you today.

I'm **praying** that you will. . .

have a **wonderful** day!

thank God for all He's done in your life!

enjoy your **memories** of the past!

and take **delight**

in the future's **promise**!

Happy birthday!

DayMaker
GREETING BOOKS

© 2004 by Barbour Publishing, Inc.

ISBN 1-59310-361-1

Designed by Anita Cook. Artwork by Pat Hill.

Published by Barbour Publishing, Inc., P.O. Box 719, Uhrichsville, Ohio 44683,
www.barbourbooks.com

Our mission is to publish and distribute inspirational products offering exceptional value
and biblical encouragement to the masses.

Member of the
Evangelical Christian
Publishers Association

Printed in China.

5 4 3 2 1